I0151475

Sinking City

poems by

Noah Renn

Finishing Line Press
Georgetown, Kentucky

Sinking City

Copyright © 2019 by Noah Renn
ISBN 978-1-63534-836-1 First Edition
All rights reserved under International and Pan-American Copyright Conventions.
No part of this book may be reproduced in any manner whatsoever without written
permission from the publisher, except in the case of brief quotations embodied in
critical articles and reviews.

ACKNOWLEDGMENTS

"The Longest Beer Ever" and "Where to Look"—published in
Words+Pictures, 2016
"In Which I Compare My Daughter to Stars"—reprinted in *The Ekphrastic
Review*, 2016
"Built to Flood"—published in *Whurk*, 2015
"Cause and Effect"—published in *The Quotable*, 2014
"The Gun Show"—(titled "Did You Get Your Tickets to the Show? What
Show? The Gun Show") published in *New Verse News*, 2009

Publisher: Leah Maines
Editor: Christen Kincaid
Cover Art: Sargeant Memorail Collection—Norfolk Public Library
Author Photo: Leslie Renn
Cover Design: Leah Huete

Printed in the USA on acid-free paper.
Order online: www.finishinglinepress.com
            also available on amazon.com

Author inquiries and mail orders:
Finishing Line Press
P. O. Box 1626
Georgetown, Kentucky 40324
U. S. A.

Table of Contents

*"We're just at the mercy of the flooding,
sometimes you can't get in, sometimes you can't get out."*

Cheryll Sumner, Norfolk, Virginia

SPEAKING CITY

Every time I speak
the first word is the river
the next is always the bay.
The pause in between is the city.
Every breath, the hurricane wind
that bends these street signs blue.
I utter the church
where I carried a cross
and washed the feet of priests.
I spit basketball courts
where I was chosen by strangers
to share in beautiful, communal dance.
I heave out while waiting
for the 8, the 2, the 23
the bus's cold moan.
All my songs are graffiti
thrown on shipyard hard hats.
Here is the acetylene torch
the very weld that bonds the ship.
I talk in chipped bricks
stroll skylights,
I speak through this chain link,
the little-league backstops.
Holler over the bridges.
Whisper in the tunnels.
Every period a coal train at the terminal,
every comma a wave breaking West.
How can I say anything
but this city when I was raised
on the slow music of storm drains
and the silence of empty lots?
I carve all my secrets
into the crepe myrtle,

so it can shed its skin
in the park where I stomped
and got stomped, beat,
beating my way into a brotherhood
of grass and sand.
Every time I speak
the first word is my brother.
The next is always me.
The pause in between is our father,
the city, a fleeting deposit of silt.

EMPTY LOT

The deadend street where I'd spent my life
and the row of houses that stood there
were interrupted by an empty lot,
a place where a house was supposed to be.

Not a field or a park,
it just looked like the planners
had forgotten to build there.
We should be lucky they forget
to build anything now.

The favorite place for dogs
to lead their masters when walking,
where teenagers went to smoke and drink
and do whatever their parents were.

It was great for a football toss
with your brother if you had one;
you were lucky if you did.

And although the lot was homeless,
I never saw any one sleeping there.
I can recall our neighbors talking
of buying it up, and a civic league
effort to make it something
it was never meant to be.

I wonder, if I ever went back,
would I be lucky enough to see that nothing
is still there, if there might be a window
to look into, a television light,
a family eating together.

WEIGHT OF ALMOST

It's wireless light,
like signals over oceans

and bearable. It's like when I'm almost
finished grading essays, cleaving

the column of papers that have
collected sawdust in manila

envelopes. And then the weight
of incomplete thought returns.

It's when my lighter
is almost out of gas, when I can only

draw a blue flame, the color almost
hot enough to ignite

when I just want to smoke
in an alleyway, to see

a cloud rising up
and over my head. It's light,

like how I know the smoke
will settle elsewhere.

And it can also be heavy can't it?
The air in the room of the almost

dead, when I'm not sure if the weight
of tears is enough for gravity

to extract, when my wife is almost
ready to bear a child, body swollen

with life almost to capacity,
when change is almost everything.

BUILT TO FLOOD

You may have let your dog lead you to the park,
or be waiting for the light on Delaware when you see
six skateboarders kick-flip and shove-it
down the long war of parking lot where the city drags
its shoulder along the water.

You may notice the holes in their shoes, worn
along the outstep where the river might seep in,
plus the ragged plies of their boards.
One young man slides away from the rest.
Jumps the gap of creek stone.

A storm over the trees, and you dare
to think how quickly the Elizabeth can rise.
By the time he points East at a moon that's out
during the day, you've watched the light turn green,
stopped counting the others who are already gone.

COLLEGE BAR

Laura really likes Mexican guys.

I ask the bartender where I can get one of those
Jim Beam shirts he's wearing, and order another
to show how much I love the product.
Maybe he'll give me a shirt I think,
or I could've just wanted to use my own voice
to drown out those coming from the bar:

> *I didn't want to make it awkward. But.*
> *Laura was being really skanky,*
> *and so I didn't say anything about her baby.*

And I think, this is pretty damn
awkward for me, here at the bar
by myself—school official and all that,
swilling it up with the cheetah-print-clad student body
when I realize I should be in workshop now,
telling people what I think about their writing.
But.
My baby is with the sitter.
My wife is off in a war.

The sushi at Sakura tastes like rotten mushrooms.

A thick shot of Kentucky straight
bourbon whiskey makes
an offensive through my torso,
attacks my abdomen.
Someone gushes over a word,
or sits confused.
Another captures the ether
in a loosely bound notebook.

EVERYTHING WEST OF NEWTOWN
—*for Bean*

It's time to redraw the borders.
Said everyone losing their latest game of *Risk*.

Bean said, *have you ever even seen a map?*
The world is big, man.

Uzbekistan posts up on Kazakhstan like somebody
sticker bombed its dumpster fence.

Italy's not a boot.
It's a tree with a magic door.

I can't even explain the two Georgias
without confusing somebody.

Our city ain't nothing but silt on a seabed.
Every time I sneeze I feel it shift.

Even when the floodgate fist bumps the bulkhead
the river still spills its fast love.

All we know is it ends
where the street signs go green.

And our dad had no boundaries.
If they'd let him tape-off the world

he'd cop an avocado farm
and measure by pepas de aguacate.

I want to see the sand on the sidewalk in San Juan,
and remind polar bears about their fathers' glaciers.

But Bean's never chanced the Atlantic
or even hit the midtown tunnel save for funerals.

If we ever leave this place, here's what on the line:
An evil inheritance of hearts

heat checked at absolute zero,
the miles of wire we ran

through the mall, our initials
—deemed gang graffiti—

in sidewalk concrete,
one JV championship trophy,

one DUI, our mother's empty home,
two of the world's most unfinished stories
starting over again.

DRAIN PIPE

Either the head or the tail of the storm system,
the drain pipe out in Pretty Lake
revealed the city's insides like the skin of the land
had peeled back and exposed its middle finger bone,
so it could flick off any one standing at the wrong angle.

As kids, we'd walk all the way to the end, lay down
to dirty the chests of our shirts, hang our heads low enough to see in.

Then one of us would dare another to enter,
testing our young man-limits and fears.

Some would just dangle there and wonder what death
was coming out or going in.

Others dropped down, dabbling their shoes in the brown sludge,
but would go no further than where the light stopped.

One time, when no one even said to, I went so far,
and stayed so long my friends called out to me
scared I had slipped or gotten lost.

I can remember it was not so bad down there.
The tube was warm from the earth. The air was clean.
With water at my ankles I surfaced through a manhole,
and walked straight down my street, as if now I knew
everything that was beneath me.

WHERE TO LOOK

Route 17 traffic pumps southbound through Nelson county.

The hills an impossible green as the cars close in on the next city.

The drivers begin to hear each other's music.

Two-thirds of these people are listening to love songs.

Up above them all, in sky too-blue for this time of year—

the early spring a result of the earth's decision to tilt

before everyone was ready—

seven hawks hang aloft.

Four of them are already stuffed with their share of field mice.

One house has a metal roof and a barn

slowly succumbing to gravity.

A man on the roadside pinches his finger lifting the hood of his truck,

overheated. Roughly one pump's worth of his blood is sent to the site,

if for anything—just to indicate where to look.

OFF GRANBY ST. BRIDGE

If you're from here
you may think you know its brackish tide,
But to jump into the Lafayette is to feel something
alien-- an odd instance when you ask:
What will come out from these depths?

As you jump
listen close to the drivers passing,
their brief gasps.
They think you might die,
but you won't. Not then.

So admire the sheen of gasoline
and its false rainbows.
Break the surface.

When you land
let your ankles tangle
in the silt's tentacles.

Then let the ribs of your young frame
expand as you crawl South
through the sun under the bridge.

Get home and ready for work.
Tie up your black-soled boots.
Sweat out everything inside you,
let it slide back into the river.

CAUSE AND EFFECT

The fact that the blades of knives left unused for a month-or-so
return without fresh setting or sharpening is amazing,
but because no reason for this has yet been assigned,
The World's Largest Knife Outlet closes early on St. Valentine's Day.

Because I know spraying the back of my daughter's arm
lets the kiddie-pool-slosh water the grass,
and because they go unwasted
the tears from the hose can't be mine.

I thought once to tell her to sap the earth like the wisteria root
because even if it has the most wanton and wicked arms,
its purple lanterns make perfect frames for people's faces.

Because the whole of him rarely adds up to the sum of his parts,
it's sad (but not that sad) the Cheshire Cat's web page
is unavailable for viewing.

We both hear the neighbor lady's baby
crying in the house next door,
but I'm too scared to define for my daughter the word *widow*
or explain the reasons for war.

I know for a fact the collective self-bounty of Americans
has emptied out faster than a whiskey drinker's bowels
after the first sip of morning coffee, but that's not the reason
the stock price for The Paintings of Horses by Amateurs Inc.
has utterly plummeted into the valleys of those same paintings'
backgrounds.

But because a murderous psychopath now thinks
all the gods he never believed in
are a simpler human's explanation of aliens
poised to return in fits of violence and disappointment,
because now there is something to answer to—

with eyes and arms that will slide knives through him,
disassemble him into his component parts—

he has stopped killing people
and is now Executive Director
of the local nautical museum
I cry, after the pool's emptied, my child is sleeping,
and the mice in the garage watch safely
as I paint landscapes and horses and huge purple moons.

ARMY BAR
—for PFC Flannery

A Sergeant pulls on her beer
before thinking out loud about her soldier
and the circumstances of him.
Water drops hang tight then lose themselves
from the pint bottom.

Someone listens in a way that lets them think
about the condensation—
how heat always moves into cold.
A movement they never felt
when they found him.

He couldn't have been in uniform.
says the Sergeant. *Plus, it's suicide anyway,*
going full battle rattle
and headlong into orders.

I tried to commit—
make something poetic about it.
When you fight a war for no reason, I said.
You don't need a reason for anything else.

A fly near her face.
Her battles around us
shots to their lips.

No reason. To drink and drink and drink
himself into a desert-cold sleep,
or to swallow a barrel,
or to muster the strength
to string up 550 cord
between the beams and plywood
of an unfinished garage attic.

FATBACK

A hunk of fatback lies wrapped
in white butcher paper between us.

Pig from dad's fridge, a gift for his sons.
The smell of its smoke covers the distance

between angry and loud. We are brothers.
Like many American men we argue

about women, war,
and the declining value of things

like paychecks and hard dicks.
In the back seat sit our children,

and somewhere in the screaming
he says his knowledge is better than mine

because college isn't the real world.
The state line approaches, a Confederate flag.

The fatback's aroma sits in our clothes
and in the car like dad was still with us.

The baby cries a song to the corn growing
along the road while two men fight over nothing

and everything.

IN WHICH I COMPARE MY DAUGHTER TO STARS
—after the painting "Young Woman" by Mike Brewer

My daughter's red hair is so startling

people stop us

walking home from school,

in the grocery, while she hangs

on my arm in the mall, just to mention

how its color—like the fresh heat of a protostar—

has affected them.

So, she already knows the power of a stranger's attention.

I am startled, in front of a painting

that has propelled me light years into the future.

Where a young woman, my daughter

has turned her head toward a man.

Her neck has expanded,

to hold everything I've taught her

plus the weight that comes

with the gravity of growing up.

What does she know now?

Of the man who for hours

stared at what she's become.

What does he know of her?

How, when she was young enough to hold

her mother sang to her on a porch swing

as the universe swung in unison.

Yes, there is the best mix of blue and grey

to splash the galaxies of her iris.

The skill to draw wire across her frame,

so she may hang on a gallery wall.

Here, years from now

strangers see her elbow point west

toward a source of dim light,

her hair—hot red, the core of the sun—

and again feel compelled to stare

and say something.

ALTERED BEAST

My brother was a monster
when he believed he had dominion

over our TV, our house, our time.
Time got distorted

as he battled with demons and undead
for hours, ages trying to save a princess.

Like in most games he started off a normal guy.
With some dark magic he became

half a wolf, bear, tiger
half a man.

When it was time to eat,
the attack happened.

It was less that he was greater than himself,
more that the human inside was lost.

—Mom cut off the power—
His palms slipped with sweat.

Reason slipped out of the den.
The control was unwieldy

when he threw it at her head.
Blood.

Then I watched the terror
of his act descend.

GUN SHOW

On my street,
yes, the same street with the empty lot
and the drainpipe that looks like a middle finger
sticking out into Pretty Lake,
people had guns.

Scott's rusty revolver in the Phillies box.
Dale's .45 cal top shelf closet.
Esco's sawed off in the trunk.
Jessica's twenty-two in the knock-off hand bag.

When I got my first one, I kept it on me.
And you don't have to believe me, but
I have changed since then—
since I used to smoke in that empty lot,
since I climbed into that drainpipe
and came out a manhole up the street.

And I don't want to be like that
young kid who shows off his Glock
pulled from the sag of his jeans
and grey hoodie
and points it at you—
but just for show.

I want to be the old head, and less drunk
off the idea of killing people.
I want to be the one to tell him
to put that shit away.

#REALTALK

If you met me at a cookout—
you'd think I'm a guy who smiles too much
someone who makes less money than you,
but whose children are more beautiful than yours—
and if we'd strike up a conversation
you'd say, *Real pretty day.*
And even though I'm a guy who thinks
there's not much difference between pretty and *real* pretty,
I would still talk with you as politely as new neighbors do.

But by the time the cheese goes on the burgers,
and another guest speaks candidly
about not making his mortgage this month,
I might want to ask you
why you said *America's gone be better off*
now that we got rid of that Black president.
And that was *real talk*—
like you didn't know we were standing
in a city that's half black.

And if between sips of their hand-warm beers
several others emphatically agree,
and add that the mere presence of gays and Mexicans
account for the rest of our nation's *real* problems
I might want to call attention to the sad point
that you and your partiers' over use of the term
renders it meaningless.

At dusk when I tell you what I do,
you'd mention you don't care for poetry,
its tendency toward big words.
That's just not how real people talk. You'd say.

But if I were to write a poem about you,
I'd be real—at least in my admission
that some of what I write is made-up.
And I will point out that in reality, whiteness and maleness
are as fragile as the bottles in our hands.

Because, as the charcoal briquettes release their final heat,
I might realize—a poem is a yard with a burnt-out stump
where the truth about ourselves leaks out as the sun goes down.

DISTANCE
—after Georg Wilhelm Friedrich Hegel and Bette Midler

Since I've found the courage to rethink everything,
to see the world from the sky or from space or any place
other than the old block I grew up on,
it doesn't look so good. The flesh of the earth is stripped raw,
ice caps are chipped paint, a city-island of trash churns in the ocean,
and it's obvious there is too much war and too many cars.

See, when I was young and didn't have to pay attention
to missing radii, points of stars, or the systemic evil of the world
I used to confuse the Mercedes Benz symbol for the peace sign.

Now I can only think about glaciers,
their grand movement across the earth—
and what we've named their march. We say advance, retreat
like a glacier is some abominable army of time.

As a teenager when I'd drink at the deadend
of my street, knee, chest, shoulders
deep into ungodly volumes of alcohol
I would realize car makers' malevolence,
and how badly the ice is losing its battle.

Watching the water in Pretty Lake
invade the boundary of the city, I know
it is sinking, and now, at least I *understand*
what is happening
inside internal combustion engines,
behind impoundment dams,
I'm privy to acid rain and how it does
what it does to my patio set.

But when my backyard was engulfed
by an uncanny surge it didn't matter
who was looking, and from what distance.
I stared out, watched the bird house float away
stepped through the water
feeling with the soles of my boots
everything below the surface

That's my kid's tri-cycle
                    That's my old tire
        That's my sunken bottle.

MOLT

I was born by the river.
My children too,
like we've all been sent down
in rudiment transport—
a basket of reeds—perhaps
the city itself ready for us to leave.

Instead we've stayed
through flood and fire,
made life on this silt, mud,
cattails on our deadend street.
Every street on an island
deadends at the water.

And I'm sure someone before me
has spoken about the silt and mud
how the sun breaks a shell of clouds.

April's wet ground sinks
into August's heat and all the old
weather that changes the skin,
a blue crab's translucent molt.

And in every word, a collection
of coal dust in my nostrils
in the playgrounds of my children's lungs
on the granite sills.

Someone has traced a life in the soot,
the cattails and a small creature's forgotten body—
I am still here they say
and I love it when the train cars sing.

THE LONGEST BEER EVER
—for Brian

An asteroid came just 14,000 miles from earth.

It eyed a 15-minute window wherein it might have touched us.

What are the odds a raindrop hits the cigarette's cherry—

that chance would douse our fire from such obscene distance?

My best friend tells me his father died, hands me a Green Can.

I've heard it takes 17 muscles to smile,

43 to frown.

No one's measured how many calories are burned

holding back tears.

Infinite dust particles

collect enough water vapor for gravity

to act upon them

as we ignite .003 ounces of butane

to light our Camel Lights.

A glacier of playsand advancing

from the turtle shell rinses away in about 1 night.

Most cargo trains carry 100 cars.

It'd be tough to estimate just how many backyards

in Norfolk feel the bang and tremble

of those containers reaching the river.

Even more difficult is counting

the shwills it takes to listen helplessly

as an old grizzly howls out his last breath

trapped on the side of his own mountain.

Our fathers may tell us they are ready for death,

that there is a measurable distance between the body and its end.

Most drivers exceed the speed limit by 10 miles an hour.

99% of movie funerals take place in the rain.

I didn't know so I had to ask

What are the chances the Azaleas won't bloom in the spring?

Originally from Norfolk, Virginia **Noah Renn** has seen climate change and sea-level rise affect the city in the forms of increased flooding and gradual subsidence. Before getting his MFA from Old Dominion University, he spent many years waiting at bus stops in soggy shoes, going back and forth between restaurant jobs. He likes to play pick-up basketball, paint and sketch, and he sometimes drives to the Blue Ridge mountains to camp. Now he spends most of his time teaching and taking walks with his family. His poetry can be found in *The Ekphrastic Review, Whurk, 30 North, Blue Collar Review, The Quotable,* and *New Verse News,* among others. His nonfiction can be found in *Cezanne's Carrot* and *Full Grown People.*

www.ingramcontent.com/pod-product-compliance
Lightning Source LLC
LaVergne TN
LVHW051614080426
835510LV00020B/3289